For Peter Stitt,

In appreciation for your work.

Best wishes,

Daniel McGuire

10/22/82

The Common Life

poems by
David McKain

Some of these poems have appeared, or will appear soon, in the
following magazines and anthologies: *The Ardis Anthology of New
American Poetry, The Bellingham Review, The Centennial Review, The
Colorado State Review, Connecticut Artists, Connecticut River Review,
Connecticut Writers—1979, Contemporary Anthology of Poetry, The
Fiddlehead, The Greenfield Review, The Greensboro Review, Harvard
Magazine, The Kansas Quarterly, The Minnesota Review, Modern
Poetry Studies, Passage, Phoebe, Poetry East, Poet Lore, Poets On,
Praxis,* and *The Unrealist.*

I would like to thank Yaddo for the opportunity to write without
interruption for the better part of a summer and, too, the National
Endowment for the Arts for a 1981-1982 NEA Fellowship.

Jacket design and illustration by Jon Friedman
Photograph by James Holzworth

Typesetting and production by
Ed Hogan/Aspect Composition

The publication of this book was made possible with support from the
Massachusetts Council on the Arts and Humanities, a state agency whose
funds are recommended by the Governor and appropriated by the State
Legislature.

Library of Congress Catalogue Card Number 82-071818
ISBN 0-914086-38-3 (pbk.)
ISBN 0-914086-41-3 (cloth)

Alice James Books are published by Alice James Poetry
Cooperative, Inc.

Alice James Books
138 Mount Auburn Street
Cambridge, Massachusetts 02138

For Margaret

Contents

In Search of the Common Life

The ordinary man is the most extraordinary man.
                                          Kierkegaard

Walking up Miles Hollow
I expect a logger or a man
in a plaid shirt who works on a lease—
a man who'd make shot-gun shells
or carve a bird: near here as a boy
I rode a farmer's spotted horse,
one that drank and twitched
standing in the creek.

The same jacks still thump
pumping oil in the valley—
smell it, a teacher said.
Indians discovered it, not Drake.
She told us how Senecas rubbed themselves
and drank it, back when it bubbled up
in pools on every sacred hill.
I used to know places in the woods
where it seeped up purple through the snow.

I watch a speck in the road become a crow.
By noon I see a man scything
in the shadows of a house,
his long curved sweep, aluminum:
I ask and he pumps me a dipper of water,
watching my eyes, my hand tip
and dribble wet spots down my shirt.

He refills it twice
then shows me the axe and shed,
his wood stacked for winter,
the hook where he hangs the deer:
he shows me the creek and his garden,

an apple branch cemented white.
He's eighty-three,
his wife calls him Daddy:
in the middle of the afternoon
she cuts me sweet pea and roses
and wraps them in the comics.

On my way back to town,
kids wheel by and laugh
at a grown man carrying flowers—
I hoist the bouquet in their honor.

Where the guardrails end and the billboards start,
a truck slows down, its fenders flapping:
they honk the horn and holler.

The Birdcarver

Wanting us to see more than decoys
he talks with a knife about his dream:
to free the birds that nest inside the mind,
carve them out of words until they soar.

The white cedar's nearly gone, he says,
sold for posts and fences—
that's the wood for the long-beaked shore birds,
for their hull, nothing else will do.
For fan-tail, ring-neck or mallard,
the soft white pine from Utah.

But the neck of the shore bird curves,
turns to head, then swerves
into a beak
from an everyday branch of blueberry—

that's the thing of it,
find the right day, be ready to see,
come up on it eye-level,
the exact right stem, one
you've passed a hundred times
now curlew, Hudsonian, heron.

The native white cedar,
cut it winter from the swamp,
drag it on a sled across the ice
to season a year up on stickers—
that's a big part, getting out.

Then know calls, migrations, the moon—
like anybody with wood and time,
making something out of nothing.

Sweet Green Grass

Down by the tracks after school
I watched this woman dig a ditch
for the bridge across the creek.
Behind smudge pots and sawhorses
I watched a blue snake with red eyes
crawl up her arm and strike
at *Luckies* in her T-shirt pocket.
I watched because she smoked
and other women didn't; because she spit
and had a trace of moustache
like a man; because some men said
she'd been a sergeant in the Army,
good with all the troops. Twelve,
I couldn't tell what was the truth.

One night I saw two heads on a calf
in a bottle. This truck pulled up
into a cornfield, NATURAL WONDERS
on its side in gold: for a quarter
I saw a four-eyed unborn cow
float ghostly in formaldehyde.
God had killed the thing
and put it in a jar for me,
I thought, to see—proof
He'd meant the sweet green grass
for children He'd suffered forth.

The next year in a tent, I saw Irma
for half a dollar. Dark on one side,
hard and hairy, she flexed her muscles:
on the other side, in underwater light,
she cupped a child's pale breast.

Afterwards the story grew
one of us hid and sailed a stone,
cutting the barker over the eye.
I wouldn't doubt it. He'd lured us there
then wouldn't let us laugh,
even when Irma squatted down and flashed
the parts we'd paid a quarter each to see,
even when she spread her velvet
robes and grinned at us herself.

In full moonlight
we had crouched behind her tent:
we wanted to see her walk and talk
and crawl like a reptile—
but an older boy shut us up,
"She don't do that!"

Why *she,* I wanted to know,
when you talk about hermaphrodites?
Why did we feel giddy
and ready for a fight?
But we let the mood pass,
or almost pass. It was then
someone threw the rock
and we ran, we laughed.

Iron Deer

I'm alone with the whir of the furnace.
Half an eye catches the news—
it snows in mild Connecticut.
Tomorrow the state will close.

In the Alleghenies
I remember how snow drifted
to the deer's iron belly
at the entrance of the school.

Before we pledged allegiance
the teacher warmed a can of stewed tomatoes,
poured it over bread in bowls for three of us
who went without, she thought, at home.

With ring-worm
we sat on wooden crates
in the stock room,
too embarrassed not to eat.

For lunch
they gave us free milk and raisins:
I wore cardboard shoes,
a nylon stocking on my head.

Thirty years later
now my son's eleven:
tanned and happy
he's stranded on Saint Thomas.

I can see pencil fish
forty feet down through his mask:
the whole green world of ribbon grass
waving up in slow angles off the bottom.

I can see flowering red cactus
with tongues and stamen
like feelers on a lobster:
white yachts and red sails.

And Cabana boys,
I can see them spit behind his back:
the waiters spit,
the poor and the black.

I want to say to him,
they spit because we go to war
so you can swim,
breathing underwater through your mask.

They spit because we make fish,
they spit because we make birds—
fish and birds to blow up earth:
they spit because you're American.

But for now, I let all this fester
rather than write a letter—
besides, how can he understand
the essence of a snorkel?

How much did I understand
the meaning of my shoes and ring-worm?
I boast instead about the blizzards
I remember as a boy—

how the iron antlers of the deer
stuck up through the snow
like a child's empty rocking chair,
perched by itself in front of school.

Good Soldiers

Mornings before school, kneeling
to pray, my father read me the Bible:
he liked the letters Paul wrote the Greeks,
especially First Corinthians, Thirteen.

Lifting and lowering his voice,
chanting, he sang out these warnings:
a child should not speak as a child,
a child should put away childish things.

I had rocks and string on the floor
and thought I'd never grow another inch:
my voice would sound like eternal brass,
would ping like a tinkling cymbal.

Charity, he preached, meant love, abstractly—
in reality it was The Salvation Army:
they found shoes and clothes to fit the poor,
and Thanksgivings, they gave away free turkeys.

Before Christmas on Saturday nights,
starting at five o'clock, my mother and I marched
downtown to Woolworth's. I rang a hand-bell,
watching the shoppers drop their coins

through chicken wire into a bright red kettle.
My mother played an organ wrapped in chimney paper—
an imitation brick with a roof-top mantle of snow.
Together we worked the front exit, singing carols.

We wore navy blue uniforms and a cap
trimmed with red ribbon—everyone saw us
and smiled. Under her breath and smiling back,
my mother said they were the salt of the earth—

meaning dirt farmers who'd quit third grade,
like Eddie Berger's father and John Titus.
We prayed for them and others at night,
hoping they'd take up *War Cry* and fight.

After the store was dark, we trudged
home up the middle of the street, avoiding
drifts on the sidewalk: still the snow
flurried down, blurring the street lights.

I squinted until each light became a halo,
thinking of God and His Light, His Silence
and Snow. I thought about how the snow muffled
our boots as we marched back home from battle.

South Mechanic

At dawn the snow's mauve light began
to blue. It blurred above the trees
and fell so hard I thought of freedom—
at five-thirty, no one owned the street.

I was first on South Mechanic, first
to smell the snow and taste its iron;
at Elm I saw Richie Merrie's father
waiting for a ride to Kendall.

Up close he smelled like *Red Man*
and gun oil, like wool when it's wet;
he wore a red and black jacket,
a deer license pinned on back.

I wanted to tell him about a place
on Quintuple, a flame that burned all night;
beside it, even winter, grass and flowers
grew inside a brain of yellow ice.

But he stood there ordered in his space,
never looking up or down the street;
he just pulled himself up on the truck
listening to his hands and feet.

For two years I thought of his hands
as he shifted the black bucket, wedged it
between his knees to pay me for a paper
and then tore off a chew of tobacco.

I wanted to be like him, to drill for oil
and smell like *Red Man*—before anyone
else woke up, to stand out there
and claim the blue light of the morning snow.

The Freight Yard

In cardboard Sunday shoes
I cut across the freight yard path
to see the men who slept there.

There were stacks of iron scrap
and iron hoops; curls that rusted
on the tracks like spots of blood.

The depot was a corrugated shell
peppered through with gunshot holes
that festered rust through every riddle.

The Carboni's lived in a tar-brick shack
trimmed crimson at the door and roofline.
In front, the Virgin stood in a bathtub

tipped up on end, alkaline-blue and peeling.
Crates and wooden pallets fenced them in;
their rusty gate had been an iron bed.

The night the women sobbed, a searchlight
mounted on a flatbed probed the night
for Germans. I could hear the sirens

when a neighbor woke us. In the middle
of an air-raid drill, Mrs. Carboni had seen
a miracle—the Virgin glowed a pale blue,

flooding the freight yard end to end.
Cordoned off by volunteers, we shivered
in the dark a half a block away: then

we heard it was over, the depot black.
Touching the eyes of those who wept, a priest
nodded, a pocket flashlight in his hand.

Standing next to the flatbed, I watched
the giant light melt snowflakes in its path,
raking deep in the sky for foreign planes.

Immigrant

Under bevelled glass
they tinted his cheeks peach melba
in a gold-leafed oval frame;
then hung him in the music room,
stiffly, his collar turned.

I never saw him any other way
but my grandmother claimed he'd listen
to us sing around the Steinway after supper;
and when we sang "I walk in the garden alone,"
she'd lift her eyes to watch him smile,
smiling back through each refrain.

It's hard to believe he's gone
she'd say, over and over telling his story—
how he'd crossed the ocean all alone,
fourteen, down where they packed the cattle.
And how in five days from Ellis Island,
he walked to Snow Shoe, Pennsylvania,
with a knapsack and a satchel.
It reminded him of Cumbernaud
so he called it home. His brothers
and sisters sailed steerage later,
digging in the same rich vein with a pick
and mules. Once bent underground,
he shouted Praise the Lord for Mules!
They treat the Scots like slaves!
The Downhomers sign us up on scrip,
then rent us a shack in a patch like Wales!

So he saved and made a killing in the market
and built a house with fourteen rooms.
But all the time I watched his face

above the fireplace grow redder,
I could feel the heat of his anger.
Coal-miner, preacher, baritone—
money and salvation weren't the answer.

Coppers

Swatting spots she called flies
my grandmother rocked in her bathrobe:
at war, she flattened tin cans with her heel.
All winter long we huddled in the kitchen:
"The world makes sense," she said.
"Just clean your plate. It won't rain."

She knew how to hang green peppers,
wallpaper, and an axe to its handle,
swelling the hickory in a bucket overnight.
She grew potatoes under straw without a Book
of Glossy Giant Peas. We all saved string
and stuffed rags around the windows.

Floodtime I hung out in the woods all day
waiting for a sign the Lord had made
the river swell, combed the grasses down
and drowned the rows where buckwheat
sprouted with the corn. The yellow water
chased the copperheads uphill to town.

The poisonous snakes were everywhere.
They hid beneath loose cellar stone
and curled inside a broken bucket by the well.
But when we found one in a grocery bag
the men strapped on calf-high leather boots
and shouldered long-forked poles and guns.

My fingers in my ears, I ducked
across backyards to hear the shot
and watch the thin blood trickle down
the scales of the writhing belly.
One copper, one shot. From the men
I learned not to torture, not to waste.

My Father

Ten, fifteen years
I've told this story...

how it's winter and time for supper,
how he's not home:
my mother says, "I wonder what happened,"
knowing he'll come back bandaged
and smiling, his face ashen.

A big man, he'll use little words:
"I slipped on wet bricks,
I slipped on leaves."

Meaning he'd had a spell,
the family word for fall
or fit or interlude—

the way you lose two seconds out of life
everytime you sneeze: we'd say Gesundheit
or God Bless You, bringing back the time
a little death was nothing.

Once I was there:
we were walking downtown at noon,
the sun so hot it made the blood
film over like the top of pudding.

I could see him frowning first,
trying hard to focus,
his eyes swam, pulling him out—
then two hundred pounds,
his head bounced off the curb.

My small handkerchief was nothing.
His was yellowed from a summer cold.

Overhead,
I heard people form a circle
while I looked at knees.

The policeman stared before
wading in to sit him up,
my father's hand still fluttering
near the buckle on his belt.

I've told the story to everyone
to bring back what I'd felt
kneeling six inches from the ambulance,
from the man whose eyes were mine.

But I still don't understand:
why does a father fall downtown
on a summer day and rub himself
in public, the handkerchief dirty?

I've stopped, finally, talking
about it. The way you give up
wounds, trusting they'll heal,
left with hoping they will.

Distances

My teacher stood in front of the class
by the stars and snowflakes
and the chart that begins at the beginning:

we followed his pointer left to right,
climbing down a mountain of blue gas
through yellow space to an inch
of purple hill, the first fossil of a single
cell—3,100,000,000 years old.

Then after smaller mounds of pale grey—
after dinosaur, bird, and whale,
he came to the joke he saved for the end: man.

"Man is not like a fish out of water,"
he laughed in scorn. "Man is. We are."

He screeched in chalk one million, one billion,
and the number with twelve zeroes
to prove the distance to the stars.

I saw a whorl of white petals and three leaves—
trillium in flower by the brook in May.

And the stars were close by,
just outside my bedroom window:
I'd seen them shoot and fall
when everything else was far away.

The Death of Six Horses

With a front one hundred clipped like Pebble Beach,
the child in the family starved their horses:
six roans slumped and bloated in the barn
like baby grand pianos fallen on their sides—
legs straight out and stiff, black lips
curled over rows of yellow ivory teeth.

One teacher called the owner's daughter
"dutiful" in school, meaning blind and outraged
the way a grownup feels driving home at night,
wanting to swerve into the coming lane,
mocking life and death, defying blood
and the downward pull of earth.

Before it happened, you could see
the plush lawn with sprinklers gone beserk
hurling rainbows at the sky;
the American gilded eagle
poised on the gate to kill;
and the perfect chestnut horses, careless,
browsing gently by the fence.

God's Robin

From anywhere on the street
you can look in my eyes,
you can see what I'm thinking.

I am like an old man who asks
the meaning of fire and peace
in December, the lessons of a bird.

As a boy, I hurled gravel at the sky
to hear it sprinkle on the roof,
squatting by the garage in the dirt.

I'd fling the showers in the air
hiding my eyes. I liked to hear it
rain small stones on my shoes.

Soon there were scabs under my hair:
the rat's nest would stay, wouldn't
comb. I liked the danger, the fear.

I killed honeybees and bumblebees,
then I killed a robin. It was eating
a worm in the yard across the walk.

I heaved a sandstone, smashing it
on the flagstone like shrapnel.
A splinter stuck in its head

spilling it over, making it spin
before it twitched, before its eyes
membraned over with yellow film.

Thirty years later, a new robin
lights in the yard. Each spring,
back home, it cocks its head to stare.

Connecticut Zen

A carpenter here tells a story
how his Master said,
"Let me see your hammer"—
then sawed two inches off the end,
handing it back, handle first.
"I can see by the way you hold it,
you don't need the part I cut."

At the end of the day,
the same Master Carpenter
gave Gordon a pocketful of nails. "Here,"
he said, "you're new at this trade,
take these home tonight and practice."
Looking back fifty years, Gordon laughs.

We all laugh,
four of us holding hammers, building
a house for my wife and children and me. "Hey,
tonight let's throw a dance to celebrate!"

I look out at where we are,
out in the woods with no walls, no ceilings—
coming from stars and paper lanterns,
the pavilion fills with music.

Gordon saws across his arm, playing fiddle:
heavily comes Rick, heavily comes John—
they stomp their boots on the plywood deck,
they stoop to bow and curtsy in the middle.

Four of us do-si-do,
we whoop and holler,
honoring after lunch.

Homestead

The shadow of the hawk leaves zeroes on her skin:
she watches it curl and saddle the house,
blotch broadside down the barn and stain.

She's seen a man under the crawlspace dozing,
then climbed the hill behind the house to meet him:
she's burned potatoes for supper and stood there by the stove,
dangling a smoking pot, not speaking.

I tell her when I was a boy
a birthmark on my back spread like strawberries,
not to worry, zeroes mean nothing.

I tell her, in-season or out,
the law is on our side, I can shoot
whatever threatens us—deer, turkey, hawk.

But when a shadow slants across the porch,
she swipes her hands on her apron screaming:
she wrestles for the gun and throws herself between us,
between me and any wild thing she's come to love.

Getting Back

She slammed the lid on the washing machine,
slamming the clothes in one by one,
even the trousers, lifting them up over her head,
then flailing them into the wash, clicking
the buttons against the side. A voice
out of calm and wisdom, I tell her,
"A metal button could chip the porcelain."

Wearing the fuzzy bathrobe, the funny one,
she stormed upstairs dripping footprints,
a towel around her head; while she blowdried
her hair in the bathroom, I could have squatted
outside the door in silence. I could have watched
her, played out the chain and wound up the bear
bobbing herky-jerky, its arms ready to hug.

I could have walked stiff-legged and mocked
my wind-up toy until she laughed, angrily
at first, pummeling my chest, then laughing
in earnest, falling into my open arms.
Clowning around, I could have gotten us back.

Final Solutions

Given they had to kill,
they stand nearly off-hand on camera:
there's a bulldozer back there by the ditch
and some steer keeled over in the dirt.

I think of when our cat got sick,
dragging behind the house to eat tall grass:
after a day or two
my father wrung its neck.

With unwelcome new-born kittens he'd take
the whole litter, jam them in a burlap sack
with stone, and throw them in the river.
They were better off, he said, asleep.

My uncle raised chickens. He'd stuff them
in a funnel so the head stuck out—
with one quick stroke, the head splashed
in a bucket. We plucked the rest for soup.

Old Mr. Watson, if the moon wasn't full
and his dog howled, he shot him.
Where he grew up, Quebec, men fought
horses with their fists—sticks, pipes, knives.

But for the skilled, the high-percentage death,
no one kills better than the rancher:
he shoots cattle point blank by the hundred,
then bulldozes the bodies into a pit.

On the six o'clock national news,
he speaks in cat's ass logic—
beef is down,
there's been a dip in the market.

Hauling Tile

In terms of rich and poor,
the world is always ancient China—
I dream on the screened porch
and a breeze lifts through the valley.

My children walk across the lowlands
to the mountains—some green like foothills,
some snow-capped and purple.

At the summit they stop to rest—
to play in the shade of a plum tree,
to talk with the woman who bows.
I am proud they say please and thank you—
they are young and beautiful,
the old woman smiles, she remembers.

Even in dreaming
the world is ancient China—
I want them to see
the woman's bound feet.

I want them to know who built this palace
where they play in the courtyard—
there's a footnote six men died,
six men hauling fired clay up the mountain.

It says they lost their footing, falling
ten thousand feet:
despite this and other setbacks,
it says the Emperor wouldn't give in—
after two generations of tilewrights,
his manor was built.

The old woman rocks back and forth
on her hands and knees,
making the tiles shine:
she brings out their lustre,
their color of damson plum.

Condemned

Up and down a street marked Starr
the houses get marked X:
there's lath for kitchen walls,
cold water,
excrement in the halls.

The invisible hand of Adam Smith
lifts a skirt,
drapes it over a doorknob—
faces blow by,
newspapers jive in the wind.

The wind is there
The hand is real.

Door to Door for a Tenant's Union

Six days in a row below zero.
We pamphlet through a sea-captain's house,
broken to apartments.
In the hall through waterstains,
lead-base paint and scaling plaster
we could see a sinking ship.
The mocha walls and brown linoleum,
they're colors from the bottom.

We climb stairs to a cell
under the widow's walk
where a woman eighty lives alone.
She can't climb stairs and has no phone
so when we knock, she clasps her hands
and sings it's Christmas.

Inside, listening to how cold it gets
at night, we sip coffee with our coats on:
a pan of water freezes by her bed.

She says she came from Ireland
without anybody—no mother, no father,
but like a pretty penny, found a job,
a live-in housekeeper for a doctor.
They kept her twenty years.
She says this, her eyes wide and shining.

Smiling, she says it doesn't matter.
She doesn't want the trouble we call help.

Coming Down

During cognac, after too much wine,
he thought he saw a man selling newspapers,
his hands jammed in his apron
standing like a carpenter:
he thought of the carpenter they'd called
to rescue the cat from the roof,
the reason they'd come here to celebrate.

So when she banged her knee on the table,
excusing herself, he said it would bruise
the colors of stained glass—raspberry, amber, plum—
and her body would become his place to pray,
they'd speak together in tongues and laugh.
But it didn't make them happy, not lamb,
not three colors of wine, not cognac.

He still saw the man under the green stand
selling papers, and hadn't known how to tell her.
They would lie in their bed not sleeping
and she would ask, innocently, what are you thinking?
And the poverty of their lives would come down.
He'd talk about people lost to each other,
needing common ground, a common circle.
And when she'd fall asleep
he would hear the cat purring
curled at the foot of the king-sized bed.

Dealing with Nuclear Power

Last night as we walked away from our tents
and over the ashes of the field,
we came within inches of the place a mile wide,
a mile deep—the great burial pit.

It's a re-run, this dream.
We're always wandering out there looking
for small leaves to dry and grind with beth root,
searching through the rubble for a spring.

Or when I'm trying to reassure myself
we have all we need, we look for a bowl
to hold eggs or butter, a painted pitcher,
something perfect for the kitchen.

The spirits of the place have climbed the trees
and covered their mouths to keep from laughing—
we're that helpless. I tell my son I pulled a kayak
through eel grass, just escaping a marsh.

It seemed to take all day, until a hundred yards
around the bend, the narrow water opened up—
one by one Canadian geese lifted their wings,
bending the hemlocks down to earth.

For a moment I sat with the spirits
looking down as we skirted the pit:
there was double joy in this, looking down
through the branches, and looking up.

I tried to reassure my son by telling him
the story of the wonderful geese,
as though the yellow eyes we saw would change
with the night to day, simply by telling a story.

My son wouldn't believe it though, content
to be frightened by the yellow eyes: "No matter
about the heavy geese," he said, "it's pitch-black
out here—we need food and water."

Seeing at Night

Walking back through cedars
I think of Ryder:
midnight, pitch-black.

I learn to stare at stars
to see the path—
when it vanishes, stare back up.

In this ricochet of light, there's
an aura around each tree, each star:
I can pick it out.

My eyes work like stars
reflecting beams,
bringing light to earth.

From stars to earth,
these woods, the path,
they shake the darkness like a match.

Witching

The man who witched brought three sticks:
one like a breastbone from a giant crow,
one a cherry slingshot, forked and polished.

The third was wired, broken at the union
by a pull beneath the earth against
both hands. He showed me callouses.

We hiked in where I'd seen the buck
standing on the quarry ledge, up ahead
the rise of cedars where we built the house.

Stumbling over roots and branches, he
pitched behind what seemed a walking plow.
He held the handles of his stick mid-air

without a steel cutting edge or horse,
then cursing, flung the rod aside to rub
his blistered palms. People here say

by now he's fooled himself. He grabbed
my hand, cupped it over his to feel
the quiver, the heat of the broken stick.

But when he asked if I believed in dowsing,
I couldn't say I did. I said I believed
he had a map inside, hidden lakes and rivers.

I said enough to make him laugh and get me
off the question. Even now, drinking water
from the well, I think he knew his craft

and how to shuffle through the leaves, arms
straight out like a sleepwalker. In stutter
step, shake and stagger, walk high on water.

Fireflies

for Megan

I've combed the local bazaar
looking for a hand-carved man who climbs a ladder,
an Indian doll hand-sewn from felt and leather—
any toy and talisman stitched or whittled by hand.

I found a book called *Bird, Beast and Flower,*
gold-leafed like Chapman's Homer,
the illustrations technicolor—
I gave it to my daughter.

In the middle of the living room,
drawing with magic markers,
she makes owls from it,
deer and rabbit and the common turtle.

In black and white,
what stumps her is *pyralis*—
how to catch that blink at night,
its nerved-up magic timing.

After supper on the porch,
I tell her that wink of light—
every six seconds—
it's a sign between the sexes.

It can't be done to please the eye.
It can't be done by hand.

Tying Trout Hooks: New Year's Day

The kitchen's hot,
I think of China:
three thousand years of one man fishing,
three thousand years of small mist.

Charlie threads a hook,
he wets the nylon on his lips:
83, cooped up,
he shakes a bit.

Snow covers the garden,
we drink coffee and smoke:
he calls up a day at Willow Brook—
he'd rather fish.

He taught me how to tie
a double figure-eight,
to loop it through the eye:
"Take your time," he said, "try."

Caleb

Up here in the middle of hills and mountains,
just to make it through the shadows of the barn,
a man will sweat to ease his mind to sleep,
drop down a hayloft shaft of dust and light
wearing sisal rope that snaps his neck—
then waking, compel an inner-life so rich
the season's cruelness can not touch him.

Winter up here goes so deep they call it closed,
meaning roads aren't plowed and if they are
the snow piles twice above the mail box.
And when he thinks it's nearly summer
the horses eat wet clover, bloating up
like zebra left to die in Africa:
local legend is you've got to jab
an ice-pick in their gut
to let out gas before they burst.

We run a double risk when voices come
from God, commands we can't afford to disobey:
like the wind that spoke to Caleb,
the man who built this house, cleared this land.

"Caleb," said God one November night,
"leave this place and walk a line
straight to Crawford's Notch to meet me.
I'll hang the moon out for your light."

And thrashing over brush with hands and feet,
he crashed his face against a rock
ten miles from home to the Ammonoosuc River:

there, red-eyed and God-drunk
he opened up his mouth to pray,
goose-stepped underwater to the bottom,
then floated under ice downstream
to wash up swole and bloated with the spring.

Man Plowing

In a patch like Appalachia
two roads near here name this place
better than bench marks and aerial shots:
that's Sam Chikun and Banjo Sullivan.

Sam Chikun and Banjo Sullivan
dog-leg through the night with worms,
with tree-toads come to drown or throw themselves
before the headlights of a car.

This morning after all that rain, haze
hangs low on the rubble walls, lifts
out of valley ponds called kettles,
holes gouged out by glacial ice and rift.

All around are steaming puddles, a distant
tractor crawling back and forth along the ridge:
a farmer silhouettes against the sky
slow motion, a speck a mile off.

Each spring I watch him harrow winter rye,
his discs catching sun like chariot knives:
but the slow arc back and forth across the hill,
the glint of steel through the mist

put the mind to sleep in rhythms of
a hypnotist who swings a silver key,
who speaks in a slow deep voice:
close your mind to everything.

Overnight

Sunday we climbed the cliffs to see
out over everything
took off without map or bird
up animal paths ending in a cul de sac
of crushed fern and field grass
the den of a buck or doe

back-tracked over walls and stumps
to a circle of stone and charred logs
and cedar poles thonged to frame
what children call a fort
a place to whisper codes and pass words
used to get us over night

in morning saw lady slippers
pink veined membranes of orchid
in Greek meaning scrotum

then up an old logging road
humped in the middle leading nowhere

this is the pleasure of getting lost
to sit exhausted in the woods
watching the dog bury his bone
as though we might come back

Memento

for Elizabeth

All bone collectors love a mountain.
On the summit, death is in the open.
There are white birds and white flowers,
white berries on the poison ivy.

We tent on top and watch three deer
nose in a pile of feathers, skitter
at our step, then white-tail into brush.
Severed, there's an owl's head

in the fluff. The eyes are wide open.
I work one lid, then the other with my thumb.
Black at first, each eye begins to cloud
as though I'd *hawed* my breath on onyx.

I raise the warm head before my face
like a mask and headdress out of feathers
toward the sky. The pinions are greyer,
the down is softer than a titmouse tuft.

Home, I boil the head and pluck the quills
out with pliers, as though I knew exactly why,
filing off flecks of dried gristle,
picking it smooth for the mantel.

Wild Azaleas

for Hobe and Jean

I've always known green things
lead a life their own:
Jump-Ups, Orchid, Wandering Jew,
the pinkshell azalea from Massachusetts—
reported to have escaped
in Peterson's *Guide to Trees and Shrubs.*

Living in nearby Connecticut
I take no chances,
my old shirts flutter in pieces
from blossoming wild azaleas
tied there by my daughter.

I follow her path across Main Brook
up a rocky spine of ledge toward Howard's:
all along the way
long stems protrude from the flower's mouth
like trumpet-honeysuckle,
its funnel designed for hummingbird.

Hanging from the branches
faded tatters of cloth mark
the trees for October
when all of us, we'll go out together
with shovels and burlap slings
to bring them closer to home and tether.

Blossoming

Sunday in the nation's capital,
cherry blossoms bloom at noon.
A woman sweeps the porch of soot,
a man in the yard rakes the leaves.

When this summer comes, and the joy
it brings, I'll sing and hear
the same dog bark I heard last year,
the same moth bouncing off the screen.

Partied out, today we want nothing more
than a Sunday spin, out past the horses
and white pickets, out past the red barns
and grand manors of Virginia.

In the morning *Post,* my wife read
this is the best, the most beautiful spring
in memory, "a bold relief of marble,
edged by a blur of profusion."

I remember back ten years
when blacks rioted and burned buildings,
when they threw bricks through the windows.
I remember when human anger bloomed,

and the fires of change burned all night:
the oily rags and smoke and sulphur,
they made the fragrance sweeter,
the dark air more sensitive to light.

The Land of Birdfeeders

for Ulises Torres

We saw blue feathers dance on the snow,
sunflower seeds and yellow corn
and hieroglyphic bird-tracks.

And in front of the courthouse where we walked,
my friend picked up a rock,
cocked back his arm to fire it
then stopped, for me, and smiled,
making sure I saw the titmouse in the snow—

then tossing the rock in the air
and catching it like an apple,
he said, "You know, this country struck me first
like a gentle place, where people feed birds
and everybody owns a birdfeeder at the window.

But in my country, in Chile,
when anybody sees a small animal,
you pick up a rock to kill it,
to smash the squirrel or little bird
to take it home to eat. Even the sparrow,
three, four of them, it's enough to feed one person."

The Accused

I met the man who murdered Victor Jara,
he woke me from my sleep.
He jogged out of the locker room
and down the stadium steps,
thinking of pork chops and wine,
of Sunday when he'd take his wife on a picnic.

This could be all he thought:
one foot up on the bench,
tying his boots like an athlete,
tucking his shirt in the mirror.

Below in the stadium,
he saw a thousand men all looking alike,
looking like taxi-drivers in white T-shirts
standing in the sun.

Standing on top in his uniform
he could feel himself growing stronger,
more handsome,
and more and more he wished the day Sunday.

It felt like Sunday, the sky blue
and air clearer than a postcard:
except for the cries and the milling,
except for one man singing.

Clicking his heels, tapping them,
he marched so he could hear his own boots:
and when he faced Victor Jara,
hate flew in the face of song.

Hate based on nothing special,
just trees, just wine,
and thinking of his wife and children,
wishing it was Sunday.

Days in the Sun

When Cavafy sketches a young man
twenty-five out of work,
you know he's talking about himself;
or someone he loved as well.

The clues are in the moral sense,
in the desperate pride of being poor:
he refuses a job for money,
a position in a stationery store.

The young man called himself a gambler,
and when he didn't win at cards or numbers,
he borrowed what he needed to eat,
what he needed to mend his clothes.

And when he couldn't afford a tailor,
or maybe even needle and thread,
there's a moment of denunciation where he strips,
flinging his clothes behind him.

At this moment he becomes himself again.
Cavafy says he'd swim or lie on the white sand
in the sun, flawlessly naked;
his dark nights are kept secret.

It doesn't matter what he did.
The poet expects us to understand;
to be out of work reduces a man
to a wild and last-ditch pride.

The Wolf Man

"Now came a street-crossing, and there the man ahead of me hopped down the sidewalk on uneven legs..."
                    Rilke, The Notebooks

This is a poem to ask forgiveness
for tracking a man who howled in the street,
for hanging back and laughing
as he fluttered and stumbled,
as he turned to scowl at a stone or a stick.

Over Woolworth's, a window opened—a flash
flew across the street like a white bird,
then banked against the dark red brick.
What sort of a life is it without a house
or a dog? I shadowed him, three stores back.

He was a Kane in Kane, Pennsylvania,
thirty years out of Harvard Med, disinherited.
Using a knife and a glass of whiskey,
a mirror propped up on a kitchen chair,
he had carved out his own appendix.

To howl, he gave a little head fake,
as though he would drive to the basket,
but then he faked all over, weaving
and nodding, his body shaking.
His mouth took the shape of a kiss.

He hopped so I could hop, and when he howled
I ducked inside a doorway to cover my mouth.
I never threw a snowball or a stone,
but I would gather my strength, now, like money.
I would press a coin inside his hand.

Christmas

So keen his ears, Bartok
heard the sound of insects
chewing under bark. He heard
the forest gnawing in the night,
the ice melt in the river, floating.

I learn to listen to silence
until it fills with sorrow. Sorrow
is here everyday. After the crow
has flown away, sorrow is like the wire.
From a distance it can't be seen—
just telephone poles, the space between.

My thoughts fly like a crow, springing
off the wire, making it twang and vibrate
like a string plucked against the sky.
Beyond all sorrow there's music.

But I can't hear insects under bark.
I see hunks of purple onion, bones,
and pink grapefruit in the snow.
It's cold enough to split the pipes
three feet deep beneath the barn.

The man who comes to help me start
the car, does he know it's Christmas?
His name is Paul, stitched in red
letters on the pocket of his shirt.

Although I watch in silence, a song
wells up: back and forth we smile
in the cold, a distance between us.

Trimming the Tree

Machete-whacking in November,
I cull out the deadwood,
releasing cedars: in January
I order blue spruce and fir
in bundles of two-fifty,
each seedling big as a sprig.

I plant them in April,
four feet apart in a clearing—
it takes eight years of sun and rain
to grow a Christmas tree,
average soil, an occasional pruning,
a slow scythe between each row.

A foot a year sounds simple,
though the state's advice is, buy
herbicides, insecticides
and poison bait to kill the mice:
kill the crabgrass,
the pigweed and the shepherd's-purse,
and maybe you'll gain six months.

They say with Simazine and Dylox
you might boost your profits,
though they don't say what the chemicals cost.

They don't say you might lose a fox
or a cow, a crow or a child.
They don't say you might murder a river
or rub out a meadow.
They just say time is money,
and money the star on top.

Starting with Cabral,
Ending with Neruda

Because no one writes of roosters
weaving their song across the morning,
or deep woods that wrap our children in fern;

and no one writes about streets with fish
stacked up like roof-tile,
and fruit like shingles by the sea:

feeling cheated, I read poets with chickens
in the courtyard, clacking and thumping
when a beggar knocks at the door.

I read Vallejo, youngest son of eleven,
the voice of bread and wine and stew—
the anger that cracks like a whip.

He rides in the car with me, listening
to the news, rolling his eyes in disbelief,
smashing his fists on the dash.

I need this friend, someone who's seen
blood in the streets, someone else who's seen
the blood of children running in the streets.

For the Children

In a painting by Breughel
a hunter sights the hart
then strings his gut.

I would put him on a rooftop
as the king rides by—or, better,
near the Führerbunker:
Hitler loved the old masters,
hanging his favorites on the wall.

Did he see
the Breughel of the hunters on the hill,
the children in the village?

He might have seen the red angle of their caps
and the cold blood deer hanging from a pole.

But in his final days
he'd stand at the window and gaze,
the winter woods a print
bled to the sash of their border.

His back to the Breughel
the hunters could escape—
they could roast their venison under a hemlock,
scratch a plan in the snow with a stick.

Later they could slip back in
to do their work—
to parade the Führer
slung on a pole like a deer
through the village, upside down
in the cold winter light
for all the children to see.

Child Learning

for Joshua

My son—when he could balance two minutes
without teetering, leaning, and falling on his face,
I'd sneak up on all fours on the rug
and curdle the air with a scream,
or pop a lunch-bag inches from his ear—

just to steady his nerves for later,
just to turn his blood to ice.

To teach him
to lead the revolution against himself
as well as others,

to feel with eyes in the back of his head
the enemy's stick,
then wheel and whirl,
kicking it into the air—

and to know each heart beat:
which one drums for war,
which one drums for dancing.

And no matter how blue
the rug between his toes,
the space between clouds
and the water between islands,
never sit blind-side to the heart,
never turn his back on the Lord of Misrule.

Bonfire

Minutes from sleep,
as though clay fires best at 102,
my fever ticks with the clock—

out walk ten ceramic German men,
crazed and brittle from the kiln:
life-sized, they stare at chairs

and lamps, the table and the dresser.
Startling them, I laugh in bed—the Führer
says, "The furniture knows too much."

And like a family near tears, in silence,
the movers surround my bed. They carry
me into the street where, out there,

all the figurines yell, "Speech! Speech!"
I promise (propped up on one elbow)
something lasting, something final.

The broken arms, legs, backs, all
the furniture's heaped in a stack. I call
on the smallest child to strike a match.

Pulling Down

Down the street
the wolf-oak splits like a bone,
pulling down wires that spit
and sparkle in flames, fizz
in a coil of smoldering rope.

And along the shore
the wind is wet and warm;
boats bob on the Sound
and nose-dive, taking water;
deadeyes hammer at the masts like bells,
like a rush of randy goats.

We should watch each other's eyes,
we're coming to a new age of tenderness.
Soon great offices will topple,
chrome and steel will melt like candles.
The crowds will bunch on a faltering train;
the old will die in each other's arms,
another baby born in the cattle car.

It will take a world of pulling down
before tenderness,
before strangers hunker down in a gym
sharing soup and a flickering candle
and static on a radio.

It will take a miracle.
It will take a disaster.

Signs

It only takes a sky of birds
to turn us back two thousand years
to the sea and a cliff,
to the unmistakable omen.
Kicking the leaves home, it feels
like the final days of empire.
Birds chatter
in Audubon's sky of passenger pigeons.
All around the earth is turning dark.

Over the cornfields
I've seen birds fly south before,
but these birds jerk a few yards
then stop, perched
in the crowns of the winter oak.

Open fields on either side,
oaks line the road:
a thousand starlings cheer in the trees.

Once I saw the natural world
in Tennyson,
yanking out a flower from the crannied wall;
or in Basho, squatting by the road
to smell the flower, his hands
behind his back, in no hurry.

Now a thousand blackbirds chant
at every window of the house—
they claim dominion.
They demand the sovereign skies.

Freedom Dream

Dreaming last night
I watched myself lift off at a banquet
to read a broadside by Schegel.
I think the name was Schegel.

I watched myself rise and anchor on a chandelier,
looking down at faces for a reason why:
it was dark at sea except for candles,
a light that dipped when waiters passed
rocking like a ship or a shadow.

With a whisper I steadied to read
starting in the middle,
                        "Listen,
whenever you must die or choose
to fight someone else's war, never
wear initials or a pin, a uniform.
Learn to fly instead,
shape your mouth like wind
and push your breath to call
whoop, whoop,
whoop, whoop."

I stopped to hold the broadside up
and show them cranes in profile—
two over two, flying in tandem,
flexing as they stretched their long necks
pushing away clouds.

The printed words had cracked and hatched
into birds that flew above our heads,
floating slow motion out to sea;
they quelled the waters
and stood the candle-shadows upright.

I had dreamed of freedom:
the waiters disappeared,
the servants vanished.

Fear

"The purer the glass, the less we see it."
Jose Ortega y Gasset

This window he calls art
looks out on the square,
a man feeding chickens from a shoulder sling—
the sun rocking on the sand,
wobbling into the sky.
Sipping tea and goat's milk
the man rests under an awning,
watching a funnel of dust far off.

At first they crawl like beetles
in the desert, then shimmer
in the square: flags go limp,
slumping across each fender.

Soldiers stand like candles
in each window of the inn.
The peasant bends down
and vanishes, stealing home
to tell his wife, "Kill the dogs!"

"The moon will be full!"
he shouts, "The Prince has come!
He-Who-Sleeps-Lightly!"

Sunday School Lesson

Children sprawl on the floor
asking if Jesus was right,
will the poor always be with us?

I tell them yes,
we must wait until the Emperor snores,
knowing there is no Emperor
and no room where he sleeps.

And when the wrought-iron gates swing open,
we must stand across the street
keeping watch as the black limousine rolls by,
and when the white glove waves behind bullet-proof glass,
we must smile on the curb like children, waving back.

And we must watch the pink oiled men smiling by the pool,
watch them bend to pick up food with their fingers,
and we must know when they plot to take even more—
with coupons and fliers and loop-holes in the law.

And when we know their secret plans,
we must wait and say nothing,
holding each other back by force

until hundreds blow on their hands to keep warm,
until hundreds of thousands across the street
are stomping their feet in the snow.

And when there can be no more waiting,
we must talk in low tones, making sure
the guards are with us and the brewers,
the kitchen help and all the gardeners.